A WISH YOU WERE HERE® BOOK

YELLOWSTONE

THE CYCLE OF THE SEASONS

GEORGE B. ROBINSON & LYNN WILSON

TITLE PAGE PHOTO: BISON IN HAYDEN VALLEY.

ISBN O-939365-31-6 (Paperback).
O-939365-32-4 (Clothbound).
Copyright 1994 by The Sierra Press, Inc.

Printed in Singapore.
First Edition 1994.
Second Printing, Fall 1999.

ACKNOWLEDGEMENTS

We would like to take this opportunity to thank the many photographers who made their imagery available to us during the editing of this title. While no single image can effectively replace the actual experience of being there, we believe the visual story told by the images contained in this volume do tell the story of seasonal change and process more effectively than what the visitor would experience while on vacation. On behalf of those who will see this book, we thank you for sharing the fruits of your labors.

We would also like to thank those members of the Yellowstone Association and the National Park Service whose assistance has helped in the creation and formation of this book— Thank You!

DEDICATION

This book is a visual tribute to the insight of those few who saw the wisdom of setting aside such a tract of land for the future, without regard for personal gain. That Yellowstone and the National Park Service have become models for more than 130 countries from around the world is all the proof that is necessary to confirm their wisdom. We can only hope our own use is consistent with this wisdom and in no way contributes to the degradation of this most extraordinary legacy.

In this spirit, let us all pledge to continue to work, and sacrifice, for the greater good of places such as Yellowstone National Park.

SIERRA PRESS, INC.

P.O. Box 430, El Portal, CA 95318

CONTENTS

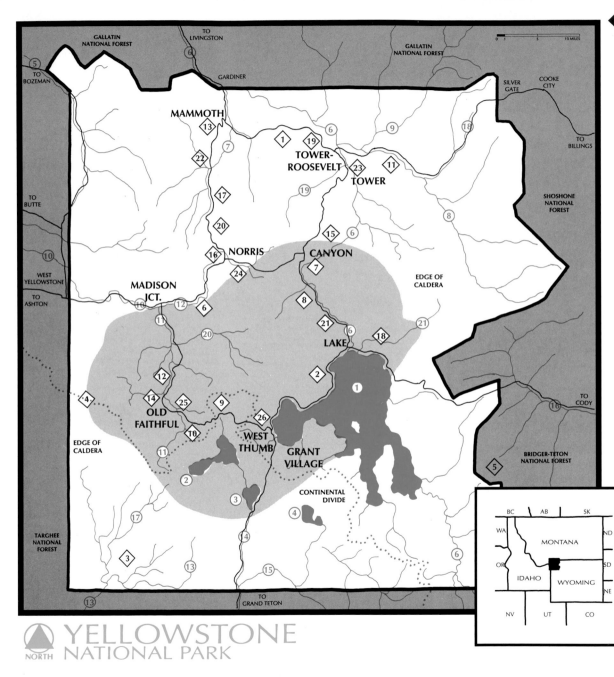

◆ ROADSIDE ATTRACTIONS ◆

1 - Blacktail Deer Plateau
2 - Bridge Bay
3 - Cascade Corner
4 - Continental Divide
5 - Eagle Peak (11,358 feet)
6 - Gibbon Falls
7 - Grand Canyon of the Yellowstone River
8 - Hayden Valley
9 - Isa Lake
10 - Kepler Cascades
11 - Lamar Valley
12 - Lower Geyser Basin
13 - Mammoth Hot Springs
14 - Midway Geyser Basin
15 - Mt. Washburn, Dunraven Pass
16 - Norris Geyser Basin
17 - Obsidian Cliff
18 - Pelican Valley
19 - Petrified Tree Exhibit
20 - Roaring Mountain
21 - Sulphur Caldron/Mud Volcano
22 - Swan Lake (Gardners Hole)
23 - Tower Fall
24 - Virginia Cascade
25 - Upper Geyser Basin
26 - West Thumb Geyser Basin

● LAKES & RIVERS ●

1 - Yellowstone Lake
2 - Shoshone Lake
3 - Lewis Lake
4 - Heart Lake
5 - Gallatin River
6 - Yellowstone River
7 - Gardner River
8 - Lamar River
9 - Slough Creek
10 - Madison River
11 - Firehole River
12 - Gibbon River
13 - Falls River
14 - Lewis River
15 - Snake River
16 - Shoshone River
17 - Bechler River
18 - Soda Butte Creek
19 - Tower Creek
20 - Nez Perce Creek

GALLATIN NATIONAL FOREST

TO LIVINGSTON

TO BOZEMAN

GARDINER

GALLATIN NATIONAL FOREST

SILVER GATE

COOKE CITY

TO BILLINGS

SHOSHONE NATIONAL FOREST

MAMMOTH

TOWER-ROOSEVELT

TOWER

TO BUTTE

NORRIS

CANYON

EDGE OF CALDERA

MADISON JCT.

LAKE

WEST YELLOWSTONE

TO ASHTON

OLD FAITHFUL

WEST THUMB

GRANT VILLAGE

EDGE OF CALDERA

CONTINENTAL DIVIDE

TO CODY

BRIDGER-TETON NATIONAL FOREST

TARGHEE NATIONAL FOREST

TO GRAND TETON

NORTH

YELLOWSTONE NATIONAL PARK

BC   AB   SK

WA

ND

OR

MONTANA

SD

IDAHO

WYOMING

NE

NV   UT   CO

A PLACE OF MANY SPLENDORS

by George B. Robinson

ISLAND WITHOUT AN EDGE

High in the northern Rockies, astride the spine of the continent, lies a treasured "island." It is a work of both nature and people.

Fashioned from the primal elements by a coalition of natural forces, it has been shaped into a place of many splendors: deep, icy-cold lakes; clear rivers, gentle cataracts, and thunderous cascades; high, barren mountains and forested plateaus; precipitous canyons stained by minerals; glacially rounded valleys and verdant meadows; and steamy, sulfurous emanations from the underground. It is a landscape energized by a volcanic heart.

This mountain "island" is called Yellowstone National Park.

Situated on a high volcanic plateau, averaging about 8,000 feet above sea level, it is surrounded by mountain ranges: the Absaroka, Beartooth, Madison, and Gallatin. In its larger context it includes the Tetons, Centennials, Wind River Range, and others. Within the park, Eagle Peak rises to well over 11,000 feet, while Gannett Peak, in the Wind River Range to the southeast, rises to just under 14,000 feet and is the highest summit overlooking the Yellowstone area.

Nature has animated it with blood, bone, and sinew; tooth and claw; green and woody tissue; fur, feather, and scale; and countless boneless bodies and microorganisms.

Cued by words and phrases, our minds summon images of

places and things, but often those images are incomplete. People are impressionable creatures. Our attention is commanded by the spectacular. The allure of the large and obvious sometimes masks our awareness of the small, subtle things without which a portrait of a place would be incomplete. Yellowstone is Old Faithful and grizzly bears. It is also lichen, pocket gophers, and beetles. The story of Yellowstone is one of massive vulcanism. It is also the story of tiny raindrops falling high atop the Two Ocean Plateau—their course to either the Pacific or the Atlantic oceans determined by a caprice of nature.

Nature is an alliance of processes—plate tectonics, vulcanism, glaciation, erosion, sedimentation, plant succession, ecological relationships, to name just a few. In Yellowstone we learn that geology affects environment and environment controls life. Here, we see the contrast between the synthetic uniformity of the world of people and the wonderful diversity of the natural world.

Secure and threatened; grand and conspicuous; small and obscure—a diverse and complex array of interdependent organisms live in Yellowstone. Here, there are aspen transformed by the alchemy of fall into trees of shimmering, golden coins; dark spruce and fir; mountainsides draped with carpets of arrow-straight pine. There are falcons and swans, bluebirds and pelicans. There are grazing bison, elk and bighorn, foraging bears, and stalking coyotes and mountain lions lurking. Yellowstone is the seldom-seen miniature world of tiny ephydrid flies hovering in the hot, sulfurous air above thermal streams, and microscopic plants living in the sunless, scalding conduits of geysers. Yellowstone is producer, consumer, decomposer. It is preda-

ROCKY MOUNTAIN ELK IN FOG, SPRING MORNING.

tor and prey. Yellowstone is a celebration of life in all its diversity, and the extremes under which it flourishes. Here, we can experience what it means for an animal to be truly wild and be reminded that we share this place with organisms that have been on the planet far longer than we have. Here, we see ecological truth: complexity and diversity are necessary for the health and stability of natural systems.

Unlike a real island, Yellowstone is not clearly defined by an outer edge. It is not confined by conventional human boundaries (lines drawn on a map). Here, the resources and their interrelationships, not the territorial imperatives of people, define the boundaries. The park is large—2.2 million acres—but it is only the core of a much greater ecosystem that encompasses as many as 18 million acres of federal, state, and private land. Animals and plants neither see, nor respect, the boundaries that people have drawn. They range throughout the larger area, so the ecological processes that connect them reach far beyond the park, like a great vascular system. Like cardiologists, resource managers know that they must care for the vessels as well as the heart. The Greater Yellowstone Ecosystem is one of the few large, relatively unaltered, self-regulating temperate zone ecosystems remaining on this highly stressed planet. But even in this high retreat, security is an illusion. The darker parts of the human shadow draw ever closer to the Yellowstone country.

Geology, fire, weather and climate, wind, water, time, and human activity are constantly at work recreating the face of Yellowstone. From immense, million-year-old geologic alterations, to the superficial annual changes in appearance that come with the cycle of the seasons, the landscape of Yellowstone is ephemeral. It is a reminder that the natural world is restless and never finished. Yellowstone is the humbling lesson that when the raw power of nature is manifest, we can only stand aside, witness, and learn.

Episodic events—from prodigious volcanic eruptions millennia ago to the epic fires of 1988—are simply nature's way of resetting the evolutionary clock. Like human history, both landscape and life are in a constant process of succession. However, while instruments of change continue to alter Yellowstone cosmetically, its essence remains unchanged. In Yellowstone we see the remarkable ability of a natural system to recover, to restore dynamic equilibrium among its parts, if free from the manipulations of people.

Native Americans, mountain men, explorers, the cavalry, the National Park Service, and visitors from around the globe have all been a part of the park's human history. In Yellowstone we are reminded that human perceptions, interests, and needs have changed over time.

Yellowstone National Park is an artifact of culture—a milestone in the conservation history of, not only the United States but, the world as well. It marks a significant change in the way people value the land. Yellowstone is a national and international icon, a gift only America could give to the world. It is a priceless estate of enduring value that we have inherited, and that we must bequeath to the future. In a way, Yellowstone is a celebration of democracy.

OF TIME, ROCKS, AND CONTINENTS MOVING
The scope of geologic time is vast, about 4.7 billion years since the

earth first took form. Geologists have divided these billions of years into four large blocks of time called *Eras;* 12 shorter blocks called *Periods;* and the two most recent periods into seven *Epochs.* We must remember, however, that in natural processes, there are neither beginnings nor ends. One cycle, one series of changes, simply blends imperceptibly into another, so the geological story is never finished.

Approximately 4.65 billion years ago, the earth and the rest of the solar system began to form out of debris from a giant interstellar explosion. The *Pre-Cambrian Era* began about 3.8 billion years ago, the age of the oldest known rocks. The place called Yellowstone came into being toward the end of the Pre-Cambrian Era, about 2.7 billion years ago. That is the approximate age of the oldest rocks in the park, part of what geologists call the "basement rocks," the ancient foundation on which the major geologic land forms are built.

The story of Yellowstone has been slowly unfolding for a period of nearly three billion years. But it was in the *Mesozoic* and *Cenozoic* eras, a span of about 245 million years, and especially during the *Tertiary* and *Quaternary* periods, the last two, covering about 66 million years, that the principal features of the Yellowstone landscape took shape.

Much of the geologic drama of the region has been enacted on a moving stage. The place we call Yellowstone is a passenger on a giant section of the earth's crust. It has drifted with the other continents, since near the end of the *Paleozoic Era,* on convection currents in the hot, plastic, upper mantle, like huge sheets of ice on a hot, planetary lake. What geologists call the North American Plate is a remnant of a single primordial land mass called Pangaea. That ancestral supercontinent was dismembered about 300 million years ago by massive tectonic forces, and the future Yellowstone began its slow, fateful voyage toward the stationary plume of molten rock that lay to the west, and to a rendezvous with human history.

The most ancient rocks in Yellowstone are pinkish, crystalline granites, dark-banded gneisses, and schists of the Pre-Cambrian Era, formed when North America was part of Pangaea. Granite is a coarse-grained igneous rock containing mainly quartz and feldspar and smaller quantities of mica, hornblende, and other dark minerals. In Yellowstone, its pink color is due to high concentrations of potassium. This granite cooled slowly and solidified deep in the upper crust. Gneiss is a metamorphic rock with thick, dark-colored streaks. It is formed when older rocks, such as granite, come into contact with superheated molten rock, or magma. Schist is a fine-grained metamorphic rock that contains many parallel grains of mica (a smooth, shiny, mineral that flakes into thin flexible pieces). Heat and pressure cause the crystalline structure and mineral composition of the original rock to change, or "metamorphose."

The basement rocks—the very old granites, gneisses, and schists of the Pre-Cambrian—have been uplifted and are exposed in parts of the Madison and Absaroka ranges near the northern boundary and extensive areas of the Beartooth Plateau, and beyond to the north and east. These surfaces, where exposed, have been eroded for millennia and present what geologists call "unconformities." An unconformity is an erosional surface between rock layers of different ages—in effect, pages missing from a book.

Sediments from the Paleozoic and Mesozoic eras were

GEOLOGIC TIME TABLE

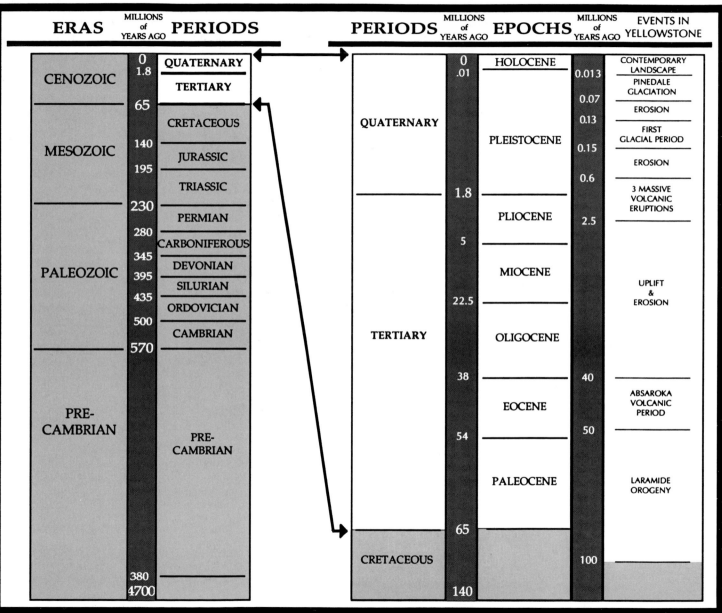

deposited on top of the worn-down, eroded unconformities. Many of these sediments contain the fossilized remains of organisms that lived in the shallow seas, swamps, rivers, and lakes that covered the region at different times.

Late in the Mesozoic Era, a period of mountain building began. Colliding crustal plates forced up the Rocky Mountain region, thereby creating its chain of mountain ranges. That mountain-building episode, only a few pages in the geologic book of records, lasted from about 100 to 50 million years ago. In the jargon of geology, this episode is known as the Laramide Orogeny.

Following the Laramide uplift, about 50 million years ago, a sequence of volcanic activity began. This resulted in the accumulation of lava, ash, mud flows, and other volcanic debris, which buried large forests that had taken hold in the young, recently uplifted mountains. The trees of these forests, many of them standing upright where they grew, can be seen today as petrified (fossilized) forests. Nearly 200 different types of fossilized plants have been found in those ancient forests.

The great diversity of species in the fossil forests is an indication of differing climates in earlier geologic periods. Strangely, the stone forests include temperate, cool-climate species like spruce, fir, and redwood as well as warm, subtropical species such as laurel, magnolia, breadfruit, and even a relative of the mangrove. In addition to trees from these climatic extremes there are those from more moderate climes, species like walnut, oak, maple, and hickory, which today are more typical of eastern hardwood environments.

The debris that inundated and preserved these ancient forests was produced by volcanoes in the Absaroka Range. Geologists

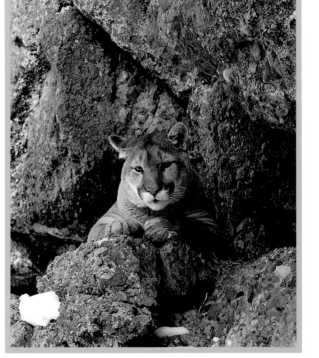

say that there were two chains of active volcanoes separated by a broad lowland, less than 1,000 feet above sea level. Subtropical and tropical trees flourished in the valley and on its margins. The higher slopes, which rose 5,000 to 10,000 feet above the valley, favored the growth of cool-climate trees such as those found in Yellowstone today. The forests were covered and "petrified" by debris from volcanoes on both sides of the lowland.

The Absaroka volcanoes stopped erupting about 40 million years ago, and there followed a period of uplift and erosion that continued until about 2.5 million years ago. This series of events was followed by another volcanic period, which lasted until about 600,000 years ago. It was during this cycle that a series of three massive volcanic eruptions shaped the Yellowstone Plateau that we see today. Those eruptions collectively ejected more than 900 cubic miles of volcanic debris, mostly ash particles welded together by intense heat into a rock called "welded tuff." Individually, these eruptions dwarfed those of Mount Mazama, Vesuvius, Krakatoa, Katmai, Mount St. Helens, and others that are usually listed as the most devastating. The last of the eruptions (10,000 times more powerful than the one that tore apart Mount St. Helens) produced what is called the Yellowstone Caldera, an enormous volcanic crater in the center of the park. It is nearly 50 miles from rim to rim. A visit to Yellowstone is a descent into the one of the largest volcanic craters on Earth.

Volcanic activity continued sporadically until about 70,000 years ago and included another, smaller, caldera collapse a little less than 150,000 years ago, which produced the basin occupied by the West Thumb of Yellowstone Lake. Also during this period, the most

recent lava flows of reddish rhyolite occurred, partially refilling the Yellowstone Caldera, forming much of the central plateau. Rhyolite is a volcanic rock that is the chemical equivalent of granite, but it forms on the surface as thick, silica-rich lava cools. Often, it is ejected explosively in dense clouds of ash (welded tuff).

The volcanic heart of Yellowstone still beats just a mile or so beneath the park. It is the hot tip of a plume of molten rock reaching upward toward the underside of North America from deep within the earth's mantle. It is that plume, or "hot spot," that generated the massive caldera eruptions, and which fuels the world's largest concentration of geysers, hot springs, and other geothermal features—over 10,000 at last count.

The gradual southwesterly drift of the North American Plate over this stationary plume of magma is confirmed by a tell-tale path of older calderas and other features extending from Yellowstone, through the Snake River Plain, toward the West Coast. Presumably, the older features passed over and were created by the same hot spot, like a welder's torch burning through the underside of the continent. The evidence resembles a series of volcanic footprints crossing the landscape. Geologists believe that the scars from the hot spot may eventually weaken the crust enough to cause the continent to split.

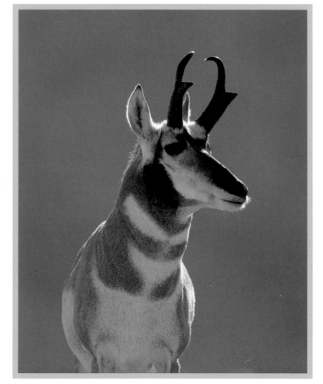

Except for the magnitude of the eruptions, and the generally east–west direction, the succession of older volcanoes leading from the Yellowstone caldera back through the Snake River Plain is not unlike the chain of volcanic islands in Hawaii. The Hawaiian Islands were formed as the Pacific tectonic plate moved gradually northward over a stationary hot spot beneath the Pacific floor. Of course, they are aligned in a south–north direction, with the oldest islands to the south.

Another indicator of the movement of the North American Plate is the infrequent release of tension along the San Andreas (and other) fault lines where it abuts the north-moving Pacific Plate.

In addition, local tension is periodically released through a network of faults that lace the region. The resulting tremors in the earth, often occur in swarms detectable only by sensitive seismographs. Occasionally, much stronger tremors (earthquakes) like the ones at Hebgen Lake in 1959 and Mount Borah in 1983, reconfigure the surface.

THE ALCHEMY OF WATER

Yellowstone, although born of fire, has been shaped by water in the form of ice. At least twice, the area was covered by glaciers up to 3,000 feet thick. Periods of cooler, wetter climate, resulting perhaps from the volume of ash ejected into the atmosphere by the earlier eruptions, were the prelude to the advance of glacial ice. It was the beginning of the final chapter in the geologic story of Yellowstone.

The first glaciation occurred sometime between 160 and 130 thousand years ago, and the second between 70 and 13 thousand years ago. It was during the later period, known as the Pinedale Glaciation, that ice scoured and softened the contours of Yellowstone (helping to create Yellowstone Lake) and deepened the ancestral Grand Canyon of the Yellowstone River. These long-departed ice sheets left evidence of their passage in the form of U-shaped valleys, moraines, erratics, cirques, and scoured rock.

Following the massive effects of volcanoes and glaciers; the gentle touches of wind, rain, streams, and rivers continue to add fine details to the landscape. Within the Greater Yellowstone Ecosystem lie the headwaters of major rivers such as the Yellowstone, Snake, and Green, as well as other watery conduits to the sea. Precipitation falling in the region is directed by the Continental Divide through those rivers into the Missouri, Columbia, and Colorado, and, ultimately, into either the Pacific or Atlantic oceans. It's like dropping water on the peaked roof of a house: it flows one way or the other depending on which side of the roof line it falls. The direction of water flow is determined by topography, not a compass. Any given watershed is usually a confusing tracery of streams. A good example of this is found at Madison Junction, where the south-flowing Gibbon joins the north-flowing Firehole to form the Madison River. The Madison then flows west, then north to where it joins the Missouri River. The Missouri then flows east, then south, to join the Mississippi, which finally empties into the Gulf of Mexico.

Approximately 10 percent of Yellowstone is covered by lakes, streams, and rivers. In addition, during much of the year, snow blankets the area. Depending on the elevation, average annual precipitation ranges from about 12 inches in the arid, lower areas around Gardiner, to about 70 inches on the Pitchstone Plateau. Whether in the form of summer rain or melting winter snow, there is an ample supply of water, which is one of the essential conditions required for the formation of geothermal features. Heat (another essential condition) is provided by molten rock, closer to the surface here than in other parts of the world, and possibly by the radioactive decay of elements at even greater depths. Pathways for the water to reach the heat source

are provided by a subterranean network of fault lines and fractures (the final essential ingredient). Heated water then rises and reaches the interconnected ductwork of the thermal basin, usually only a hundred feet or so beneath the surface. There, it collects and will eventually return to the surface as superheated water or steam, usually through a constricted passageway.

Most of Yellowstone's geysers and other thermal features are concentrated into fairly small areas called "basins." There are nine geyser basins (Upper, Midway, Lower, Norris, West Thumb, Gibbon, Lone Star, Shoshone, Heart Lake), all located within or near the rim of the ancient caldera. All but Lone Star, Shoshone, and Heart Lake basins are easily accessible from park roads. While their relative isolation helps insulate them from the impact of millions of people, visiting the more remote basins can be a wonderfully serendipitous adventure for those who have the time and inclination to venture into the backcountry.

The Upper Geyser Basin, where Old Faithful is located, has the largest concentration of geysers. In addition to Old Faithful, it is the home of more than 130 geysers and many colorful hot springs. It is where some of the more famous geysers, such as Beehive, Grand, Riverside, Giantess, and Castle, are found. The Norris Geyser Basin is the third largest, next to the Lower Basin just south of Madison Junction.

Of the major concentrations of geothermal features in the park the oldest, most active, and most frequently changing is the Norris Geyser Basin. It lies above the intersection of two major faults: one extending south from Mammoth and one reaching east from

Hebgen Lake. They, in turn, are joined by other fractures that extend outward from the rim of the caldera. It is a subterranean junction where earth-moving adjustments are continually being made. The geysers and hot springs of Norris are believed to have been changing in response to tremors originating along these faults for the last 115,000 years.

In addition, Norris is the hottest thermal basin, with a temperature of 459 degrees F., little more than 1,000 feet beneath the surface. It is also the location of Steamboat Geyser, the tallest, and possibly, the most unpredictable in the world. Perhaps no other geyser is more indicative of the variability of eruptive cycles. Contrast its spectacular eruptions (from 300 to 400 feet high and from four days to 50 years apart) with those of Bead Geyser (in the Lower Geyser Basin), which erupts every 23 to 30 minutes. Eruptions from Bead Geyser, only 15 to 25 feet in height, seldom vary more than 30 seconds from the average frequency. It is the most regular of all the geysers. While Old Faithful is the single feature most often associated with Yellowstone, it is neither the oldest, tallest, hottest, nor the most regular geyser.

The water at Norris is acidic—some of it quite strong—but in all the other basins it is alkaline. Thus, one of the most common interpretive tools of park naturalists conducting walks in thermal areas is litmus paper, which indicates whether the geyser water is acidic or alkaline. Naturalists also carry thermometers to measure and demonstrate the high temperatures in geysers and hot springs. Erupted water in all the basins has traveled perhaps 5,000 feet downward, ever closer to the volcanic heat. Water temperatures underground are very high, perhaps as much as 500 degrees F. (or higher), and water and steam temperatures in the basins are often more than 200 degrees F.—at this high elevation (averaging above 7,000 feet in the basins) water boils at about 199 degrees F.

Yellowstone is one of the most seismically active areas in North America, and thermal features are sensitive, often volatile, indicators of underground movement. In response to earthquakes, the frequency and intensity of geyser eruptions are sometimes altered or may stop altogether. It is also not uncommon for entirely new features to appear.

The lands around geysers are like living organisms. They grow. Sinter, or geyserite as it is commonly called, is an opalescent substance that is deposited by geysers and other thermal features, building the distinctive geothermal landforms in geyser basins. It is a material that has been dissolved by hot water seeping through the deep, silica-rich (silica is quartz) rhyolitic rocks that cover much of the central plateau, and redeposited on the surface as the waters cool. Throughout the park, the rate varies, but sinter is adding to geyser basin landscapes at measurable rates, usually slowly, a few hundredths of an inch each year.

CHANGING COLORS AND PRIMITIVE PLANTS

Thermal basins are not unlike the palette of a busy artist, a constantly changing blend of colors and textures. The canvas—the background color—is a whitish-gray that stands out against the predominantly green surrounding forest. Its colors are mainly from the sinter that coats it. The canvas is highlighted by kaleidoscopic accents of greens, blues, and yellows. The blues and greens are surrendered by the rainbow spectrum of the sun, causing the hot water to appear emerald and blue (like lakes and oceans). The yellows come from sulfur, and from thermophilic algae that also add hues of red, orange, and brown to the channels of water radiating from geysers and hotsprings.

Colors in run-off channels are like a spectral thermometer. The combinations of blue-green algae and bacteria (properly called cyanobacteria), which thrive at certain temperatures, tell us how hot the water is, and the temperatures generally decrease outward from the vent. Colors in the hottest waters (180 degrees F. and higher) are usually pale yellow and pinkish-white. At around 160 degrees the shades change to brighter yellows, which blend into oranges at about 145 degrees. Browns and greens begin to show up at temperatures of 120 degrees and lower. Hot springs, and the blue-green algae (cyanobacteria) that flourish in them may be a contemporary analog to the primeval environments on the young planet.

Geysers, hot springs, mud pots, and fumaroles are the signature features of Yellowstone. Old Faithful is only one of 10,000 features known to exist in thermal basins scattered throughout the park—in fact, Yellowstone is the only United Nations Biosphere Reserve to be selected for its unique geothermal features, not because it represented a biogeographic province. Save for their basic building blocks, geysers are not unlike individual life forms: each has its own specific gestation period, distinctive form, and behavior. No two are alike. Collectively, they are the largest assemblage of active geothermal features in the world. Their inconstant behavior is a reflection of the constancy of change in Yellowstone.

The inevitability of another monumental volcanic episode in the future is signaled by the uplift of what geologists call a "resurgent dome" in the floor of the caldera. This up-welling, measured at about an inch each year, is actually lifting and significantly tilting the bed of Yellowstone Lake. LeHardy Rapids, which lie above the dome and mark the true outlet of the lake, are increasing in abruptness. If this uplift continues, it may foretell a time when the lake will no longer drain to the north via the Yellowstone and Missouri rivers (finally the Atlantic Ocean), but rather to the south, via the Snake and Columbia rivers, ultimately reaching the Pacific. In the course of natural events there will, almost certainly, be another caldera formed, and its creation may dwarf the explosion that created the contemporary landscape. That future eruption will restart the geologic and biologic processes once again.

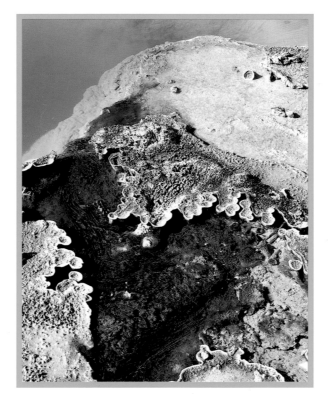

BLOOD, BONE, AND SINEW

Whatever life forms were in the Yellowstone country before the cataclysmic caldera eruptions (the most recent being 600,000 years ago) surely must have been incinerated in the incandescent clouds of gas and ash. But even in an apparently sterile, inhospitable, volcanic landscape life abides. In geologically recent time, especially since the retreat of the ice sheets, 10,000 years ago, there has been an efflorescence of life.

Yellowstone is like a huge wildlife park without moats and fences. One of the largest and most diverse wildlife populations on the continent is involved in a complex ecological drama in this remnant of primitive North America. Each species, however large or small, fills a special niche and plays an important role. Microscopic, sulfur-metabolizing organisms are no less important than the largest carnivore. All are eating or being eaten. All are connected through the

SINTER FORMATIONS, WEST THUMB GEYSER BASIN.

wonderful intricacies of natural processes, such as food chains, by which energy is transferred through the system. All are adapted to extremes of weather and climate through hibernation or migration. All are part of a grand and evolving natural experiment in which we are only late-arriving variables—transient bit players.

The fauna of the Yellowstone region is more diverse than that of most areas of the continent. While there have been some human alterations to the system, there are few other places on the continent where one can begin to experience the richness of the fauna of pre-Columbian North America. On any given day it is possible to drive for hours through pristine, old-growth forest and meadows, see large numbers of many native North American wild ungulates, hundreds of birds and small mammals, and maybe even a bear or two—something like a visit to the Serengeti Plain in East Africa.

And yet, it is not the relative richness that is important—there are many more species of wild ungulates in the Serengeti. Rather, it is the surprising integrity of the living community that is most significant. It is virtually unaltered (except along the narrow corridors of human access and use) from the time of the Native American and mountain man. This relative completeness of the flora and fauna is all the more striking in a natural world grown increasingly smaller in relation to its fabricated counterpart. With the sad exceptions of the black-footed ferret and the gray wolf, the area is believed to have a complete native vertebrate fauna, with all of its ecological associations intact. And, as this is written, there is a growing effort to restore the wolf to its former role in the ecosystem.

In the Greater Yellowstone Ecosystem there are 316 species of birds, from tiny finches to the endangered peregrine falcon and trumpeter swan. In its lakes and streams there are 22 species of fish, 15 of which are native to the area. Two dozen reptiles and amphibians are found here, among them the prairie rattlesnake, the mellifluous western chorus frog that gives voice to summer evenings, and the Rocky Mountain rubber boa, relative of the giant snakes of the tropics.

The 94 known species of mammals include all of the large North American ungulates, as well as others, ranging from the tiny and voracious masked shrew to the legendary grizzly, or "Great Bear." True to the protocols of nature, there are larger numbers of the small critters than of the large. Twelve thousand species of insects have been identified in the area ranging from butterflies to beetles, ants to mosquitoes, and wasps to salmonflies. In addition, thousands of invertebrates go largely unnoted, but are critical to nutrient recycling and energy flow through the system. In the 600 pounds of bone and muscle that we call the grizzly bear is concentrated the energy of millions of pine nuts, berries, and ants, thousands of pocket gophers and voles, hundreds of lake trout, and dozens of bison and elk calves.

Yellowstone's grizzly bear population is one of the two remaining sizable, self-regulating populations in the lower 48 states. While the population currently hovers at about 200 individuals, its place at the top of this ecosystem makes it perhaps the species most vulnerable to the fragmentation of the system. The grizzly's smaller relative, the black bear, is present in larger numbers, but neither species is as frequently seen as in the past. This is, however, not an indication of decreasing numbers. In recent years, more enlightened wildlife management policies have eliminated artificial feeding, a practice that led to the frequent appearance of bears at roadsides and garbage dumps. Deprived of this often unhealthy food source, the bears have simply dispersed back into more remote sections of the park, a much healthier situation for bears and people.

The majestic elk, or Wapiti (a Shawnee Indian word), is, no doubt, the most easily and frequently seen large herbivore. The park's elk population varies, but is between 20,000 and 30,000 at its upper optimum level, divided into several migratory herds of varying size. While historic population levels are uncertain, combined with other herds in the region, there may be about 90,000 elk throughout the Greater Yellowstone Ecosystem today—the largest herd in North America.

The largest, free-ranging population of bison remaining in North America (about 2,500 animals) is composed of three herds, which are found in the Lamar Valley, Pelican Valley, and the Hayden and Firehole valleys. Watching several hundred bison lumber dustily across a valley floor, one can only imagine what the enormous herds that once roamed much of the continent must have looked like. It is estimated that 60 million bison lived on the Great Plains, where they sustained several tribes of Plains Indians. The bison population was reduced to fewer than 50 animals by the beginning of the 20th century. The bison was saved, and drawn back from the edge of extinction in the refuge of Yellowstone. The American bison is commonly called the buffalo, a name more correctly applied to the cape buffalo of Africa. Next to the elk, it is the most frequently

observed large mammal.

Other hoofed mammals found in smaller populations include mule and white-tailed deer (mainly at lower elevations), bighorn sheep, pronghorn, and Shira's moose.

The brownish mule deer (also commonly called the black-tailed deer), like its larger elk relatives, summers at higher elevations but moves down to warmer, sheltered valleys during the long winters. Unlike the white-tailed deer (seen in fewer numbers and at lower elevations, and with a characteristic large "flag" tail), the mule deer has a short, black tail, and very large ears. Deer tend to move downslope to watercourses at twilight and early evening and can become a traffic hazard.

Sure-footed and acrobatic, bighorn sheep may be seen negotiating the steep walls of the Gardner River canyon near Mammoth Hot Springs during the winter. In the summer, they move to higher elevations. A summer hike to the summit of Mount Washburn—a rewarding trip on its own merits—may result in a surprise close-up encounter with a group of bighorns.

The pronghorn frequents the lower, drier areas, especially to the north. Perhaps more than any other Yellowstone ungulate, it looks like it was displaced from the Serengeti. It is distinctively and unmistakably colored (reminiscent of the tan or red phase of two domestic dogs: the basenji and the Italian greyhound). The pronghorn is incredibly fast—capable of quickly reaching speeds of 60 miles an hour—and can leap nearly 30 feet.

Moose are often encountered in open meadows and along stream courses. They are odd-looking creatures, whose clumsy ap-

ELK ANTLER IN THE SNOW.

pearance belies a surprising grace and swiftness of foot. Moose may be seen in Willow Park south of Mammoth, in meadows near Canyon Village and Lake, and in the Snake River area to the south.

Predators range in size from the 600-pound grizzly bear to the tiny pygmy shrew that weighs only a fraction of an ounce. Others include coyotes, river otters, pine martens, bobcats, bats, bald eagles, ospreys, owls, weasels, badgers, whooping cranes, and about 20 mountain lions. There is optimism that the gray wolf, victim of misdirected persecution and long missing from its niche in the Greater Yellowstone Ecosystem, will be restored in the 1990s. Should this occur, the portrait of the Yellowstone fauna will be nearly complete.

Nonetheless, all is not secure. There are, within the park, more than 40 species of vertebrates, hundreds of invertebrates, and more than 135 plants that are listed as rare, threatened, or endangered. Unfortunately, Yellowstone may only be a temporary haven for those vulnerable species near the finality of extinction. Even in the apparent insulation of Yellowstone, wildlife is under siege. The threat is fragmentation and loss of habitat, underscoring the need for resource managers to look beyond conventional boundaries to the larger ecosystem.

species of vascular plants in Yellowstone. Together, they function as the lungs of the ecosystem by converting carbon dioxide to oxygen.

The many different plant communities are classified according to habitat and cover type. *Habitat type* describes the sets of environmental conditions conducive to the growth of specific groups of plants. *Cover type* describes the successional stages through which a plant community passes following a major disturbance like a large fire, infestation of mountain pine beetles, or a period of glaciation. *Succession* is an orderly sequence of plant communities that occupy a given site beginning with the earliest, or pioneer species, and continuing until little change in species composition occurs—a condition referred to as the climax community.

Plant habitat types are controlled by factors such as temperature, precipitation, soil type, soil moisture, and exposure. Those conditions are largely determined by elevation. The effects of elevation are similar to those of latitude. An increase of 1,000 feet in elevation is roughly equivalent to moving 300 miles farther from the equator. While most of the park lies between 7,000 and 9,000 feet above sea level, it varies from 5,265 feet near the north entrance to 11,358 feet in the southeast. Timberline—the upper limit of tree growth—is about 10,000 feet. In addition, the vegetation is influenced by Yellowstone's latitude—halfway between the equator and the north pole.

As elevation (and latitude) increases, temperature decreases and precipitation increases, making soil moister. There are extended, cold winters, and brief, cool summers. Temperatures range from more than 60 degrees F. below zero to above 100 degrees F.

ALTITUDE, LATITUDE, AND CARPETS OF GREEN

Extensive forests of lodgepole pine as well as smaller numbers of whitebark pine, Douglas fir, subalpine fir, Englemann spruce, juniper, cottonwood, and aspen thrive in the rich, volcanic soils of Yellowstone. More than 80 percent of the area is forested, but 80 percent of the forested area is covered by lodgepole pine. There are more than 1,700

Precipitation is highest in the southwest (70 inches), where moisture-laden air flowing in from the Snake River Plain is lifted by the Continental Divide, and in the Beartooth and Absaroka ranges to the north and east, where air must rise again above the central plateau. Predictably, lowest precipitation falls at lower elevations—about 10 to 12 inches near the north entrance.

Precipitation in the remainder of the park varies with elevation, from 30 to 50 inches per year. Most of the precipitation is from snow. Fifty percent of the annual total is held in the snowpack at the beginning of April and is released to the soil during the ensuing three months. There is insufficient rainfall to replace moisture lost by evapotranspiration, so if the snowpack is low, drought conditions can develop.

Soil type is a reflection of the underlying rock. Most of the soil in the lower core of the park is derived from rhyolite, but at higher elevations, the parent material of the more nutrient-rich soils is andesite (a volcanic rock with lower silica content than rhyolite).

Topography (a result of elevation) also affects vegetation through exposure. South-facing slopes tend to have more insolation (exposure to sunlight), and so are warmer and drier. North-facing slopes are more shaded, cooler, and moist.

Scientists have identified more than 40 known habitat types in Yellowstone, of which about 80 percent are forested. Of the various cover types in the park only 15 are forested, and these are largely dominated by five coniferous species. Large areas of a specific habitat may be composed of several different covers and a given cover may extend over several habitats. Plant ecologists have further divided the park into five areas, or provinces, each with characteristic types of bedrock, soils, topography, and combinations of habitat types.

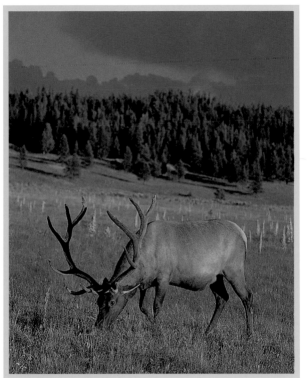

The *Gallatin Range Province* is forested with spruce, fir, and whitebark pine at higher elevations and Douglas fir at lower levels. Common understory plants include western meadowrue, fireweed, heartleaf arnica, grouse whortleberry, showy aster, sticky geranium, yampa, goldenrod, pinegrass, woods strawberry, and shiny-leaf spirea.

The *Absaroka Range Province* is forested with spruce, fir, and lodgepole pine, with whitebark pine common above 8,600 feet. Non-forest cover types include globe huckleberry, Utah honeysuckle, Englemann aster, Ross's sedge, pinegrass, elk sedge, Cascade mountain ash, and one-sided wintergreen.

The *Central Plateaus Province* is covered mostly by lodgepole pine, with scattered spruce and fir. The understory includes grouse whortleberry, elk sedge, heartleaf arnica, mosses, and lichens. In addition there are several meadows and wet grasslands.

The *Southwest Plateaus Province* is forested with lodgepole pine, subalpine fir, and Englemann spruce. Common plants on the forest floor include elk sedge, one-sided wintergreen, Ross's sedge, mountain sweetroot, mountain snowberry, serviceberry, early blue violet, tufted hairgrass, and Idaho fescue.

The *Yellowstone–Lamar River Valleys Province* is covered mostly by non-forest vegetation including big sagebrush, Idaho fescue, sticky geranium, California brome, graceful cinquefoil, sulfur buckwheat, and timber oatgrass. Forested areas are mostly Douglas-fir.

OF FIRE AND DIVERSITY

Until the summer of 1988, about three-quarters of the forest in

Yellowstone was an even-aged stand of lodgepole pine, an old-growth monoculture awaiting the cleansing and invigorating effects of fire. From the time of the park's establishment (in 1872) until 1972, there had been full fire suppression. In 1972, the National Park Service began a managed fire program that acknowledged the natural role of fire: allowing fires to burn naturally if there was no threat to human life or property. Interestingly, during the ensuing 16 years only a little more than 34,000 acres burned.

The dramatic fires of the summer of 1988, on the other hand, touched more than 790,000 acres in the park, and many thousands of additional acres in the larger ecosystem in just three months!

Large fires are known to have occurred in the Yellowstone area in the mid- to late 1700s, and it is believed that fires of the same magnitude return to this fire-dependent environment every 300 to 400 years. Populations of both flora and fauna, large and small, have inhabited Yellowstone since the retreat of Pleistocene ice, 10,000 years ago, and they have undergone many such natural cyclic events. Before the hot and historic summer of 1988, large wildland fires were a natural part of the evolutionary history of Yellowstone—for all the residents except people.

The evidence of passage of the fires will remain for a long time, but Yellowstone was not ravaged by fire; rather, it was biologically diversified, ecologically strengthened, and aesthetically enriched. Fire did not destroy habitat; it created it. Fire created community edges, and edges are biologically rich. Fire invigorated the system by reducing the old-growth forest, opening the canopy, and releasing nutrients, so that more vibrant pioneer plant species could begin the

process of succession once again. Even in areas that appeared inhospitable to life, the forest floor produced colorful and luxuriant growth within weeks—fireweed, heartleaf arnica, wild strawberry and dandelion, leafy aster, and elk sedge. Appropriately, this explosion of regrowth also included millions of tiny lodgepole pine seedlings reaching tentatively up to the sunlight, which their aging overstory would again obscure in another 300 years. Lodgepole pine is a *serotinous* species. This means that some of its cones require the intense heat of fire to open and release their seeds. In the weeks following the fires scientists recorded from 50,000 to 1,000,000 seeds per acre, or about one seed per square foot.

The fires caused little mortality among animals. Rather, they triggered an increase in various animal populations by altering plant succession and increasing nutrient forage, which in turn enhanced the availability of prey species (insects and small mammals). While there were some losses among the less fleet of foot and wing, most animals escaped injury. Any short-term loss of life was more than compensated for by the post-fire increases. Among others, the populations of cavity-dwelling birds, such as mountain bluebirds, three-toed woodpeckers, house wrens, kestrels, and tree swallows, increased. There were temporary displacements of species dependent on the late stages of plant succession, such as the pine marten, but proliferations of ground dwellers and foragers, such as the blue grouse, and general increases in predator populations, including raptors, bears, and coyotes.

The decades prior to 1988 were the last act of a long, ecological drama. The fires of that summer brought down the final curtain so that another performance could begin with Act One, Scene One. The ability to study, firsthand, the regrowth of Yellowstone is an opportunity to learn much about the successional stages of cover types and the population dynamics of both flora and fauna.

THE HUMAN CONNECTION

Toward the end of the Pleistocene Epoch the creatures that are today's most dominant and influential planetary occupants arrived in this region: humans. They occupy only the last few pages in the biography of Yellowstone. Few in number, they were probably nomadic hunters in search of ice age game. These early visitors were the first in a long procession of people drawn to the Yellowstone region. They were harbingers of a time, still thousands of years away, when nearly a quarter of a million of their descendants would live in or near the Greater Yellowstone Ecosystem, and when three million others, hunters of a different sort, would come each year.

EARLY DWELLERS

Evidence of those early humans and the groups that followed is abundant. Projectile points and the flaky debris from their manufacture, evidence of the quarrying and widespread distribution of volcanic glass (or obsidian) for arrow and spear points, and habitation sites present a clear record of human presence in the area over a long period.

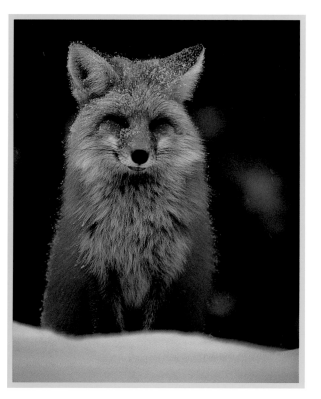

Archeologists have found evidence of several cultures that apparently evolved in response to changing climate, vegetation, and animal life. Those changes are partially inferred from changes in the type of projectile points used by hunters. They suggest, in turn, changes in the nature of the hunted. Like geologists who read the rocks and chronicle the physical evolution of the place, archaeologists have divided the human record into temporal periods that they call cultures, each with its characteristic artifacts. The presence of artifacts confirms periodic habitation in the region since about 12,000 years ago. It is in the last few hundred years that the record is most complete, yet ample evidence exists from the earlier periods to know the Yellowstone region was inhabited.

Members of several "modern" American Indian tribes are known to have entered Yellowstone during the past two hundred years, especially after they acquired the horse from the Spanish Conquistadors. Among the tribes that have connections with the area are the Blackfeet, Crow, Shoshone-Bannock, and the Nez Perce, who passed through the park during the sad flight of Chief Joseph and his band in 1877. In addition to material evidence such as tipi rings and wickiups, their presence is documented in the journals of early mountain men and explorers such as Jim Bridger, Osborne Russell, and members of the Washburn-Langford expedition.

The Bannocks were a group of the northern Paiute living peacefully among the Shoshone. One of the prominent travel routes across the Yellowstone country is the famous Bannock Trail, which was used by the Bannocks and others as they sought bison on the eastern high plains, following the extermination of the herds of the Snake River Plains.

The Shoshone referred to individual tribal bands by the principal food of the group. Thus, within the larger tribe, there were Buffalo Eaters, Salmon Eaters, Rabbit Eaters, and Sheepeaters. The Sheepeaters were the only long-term Indian occupants in the park.

Sheepeaters, probably no more than 400 altogether, in 15 camp groups, were first reported in the area by trappers and explorers about 1800. They probably arrived in Yellowstone as part of the slow, general migration of tribes across the Great Basin toward the northeast. They lived in the region for only about a hundred years. They moved their small encampments from high in the mountains in the summer to the lower elevations in winter, adjusting to the seasonal movements of bighorn sheep and the availability of foods such as small game, berries, nuts, fish, plant roots, ants, and grubs. Sheepeater homes were either simple domed wickiups made of loosely stacked poles and brush, covered with animal hides, or were roofless shelters made of a semi-circle of poles with branches piled against them. They used rocks, the hand-shaped mano and flat metate, to grind seeds and nuts into a kind of flour that they mixed with water and cooked to a mush in stone pots. Heavy and cumbersome, the stone implements were often left in the campsite, cached for future use. The Sheepeaters' clothing was made of soft, finely tanned hides of deer, elk, and bighorn sheep. They used stone knives, scrapers, fire-hardened digging sticks, and they made highly prized bows from animal horns and antlers. Their beautifully tanned hides and horn bows were sometimes traded with other tribes. They hunted mountain sheep with bows and arrows and by constructing traps to capture several animals at a time. By 1882, most of the Sheepeaters had gone to various reservations because of treaties that excluded them and other tribes from the newly created park.

While some native people may have avoided the more active geothermal features, evidence does not indicate that Indians were fearful of these areas. In fact, campsites have been found near some of them. There is some indication that they may have believed that the "steaming waters that go up and down" were manifestations of powerful spirits (neither good nor bad) that could be summoned to their aid by prayer. Warriors may have sought them on vision quests.

In any case, there is no reason to believe that these first visitors were any more, or less, awed by the geysers and other features than visitors are today.

French Canadian trappers of the 18th century wandered through much of the intermountain West, but we do not know if they saw Yellowstone's thermal features. They did travel the reaches of the upper Missouri River and its tributaries, including a river that they called the "Roche Jaune," Yellowstone. That watercourse, its headwaters high in the northern Rockies, was to become the namesake for the future park.

John Colter, a mountain man and trapper who had been with the Lewis and Clark Expedition in 1806, was probably the first white man to see the steamy, boiling water and mud, when he ventured into the Yellowstone high country in the winter of 1807–1808. Upon his return to St. Louis three years later, his accounts of the wonders that he had seen were discounted. Assuming the place he described was mythical, a journalist of the time called it "Colter's Hell."

Colter was followed into the region by other hardy mountain men, among them Joe Meek and Jim Bridger, who spent three years trapping in Yellowstone country. When Bridger returned to St. Louis with tales of a "place where Hell bubbled up," his stories were labeled

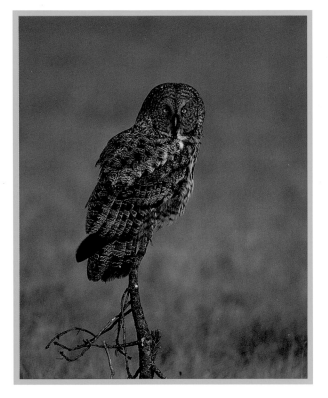

"preposterous." While he probably embellished a bit, as storytelling mountain men were wont to do, his descriptions of places like Obsidian Cliff, Alum Creek, the Firehole River, and other landmarks were not so far-fetched.

Through the journals of Osborne Russell, a trapper who spent nine years roaming the region (1834–1843), we are able to glimpse what the Yellowstone country was like more than 150 years ago. Russell was a keen observer of the land and the life of the times. Untrained as a journalist, he was nonetheless a sensitive and articulate writer who painted vivid verbal images of Yellowstone. His journals include some of the earliest descriptions of the fauna, including the gray wolf, as well as character sketches of the Shoshone and Crow Indians.

By about 1840 the near elimination of the beaver, and the increasing popularity of the silk hat, signaled the end of the trapping era. While in earlier years the possibility of finding a rich source of pelts had attracted trappers to the region, for the next 20 years the area reverted to the domain of the Indian, only rarely visited by others.

The trappers were followed, in the 1860s, by people driven by commerce of a different sort. Prospectors, caught up in the frenzy over the rich Montana gold strike of 1862, entered the area but found none of the alluring metal. In 1865, one of them, Walter W. DeLacy, published the first relatively accurate map of the region.

Beginning in about 1860, several efforts were made to further explore and map the Yellowstone country. The first organized attempt to explore the region was mounted in the autumn of 1860. A small expedition, under the leadership of United States Army Captain

William F. Raynolds, and guided by Jim Bridger, attempted to enter the area, but failed to go very far because of early, heavy snow. Other groups planned forays into the area, but none of the expeditions ever really started.

Determined to see for themselves the wonders described by others, local residents David E. Folsom, Charles W. Cook, and William Peterson entered the area in 1869. They saw most of what Colter, Bridger, and DeLacy had seen—and much more. They explored extensively and produced a much improved version of DeLacy's 1865 map. Their exploits were recounted in newspapers and in an article for the Chicago magazine, *Western Monthly*.

In 1870, a larger group, including several prominent residents of the Montana Territory, was mounted. It was led by United States Surveyor General Henry D. Washburn. Washburn was accompanied by Nathaniel P. Langford (later to become the first superintendent of the new park), lawyer Cornelius Hedges, and Truman Everts, along with a military escort under the command of Lieutenant Gustavus C. Doane.

Reports from the explorations of 1869 and 1870, a speaking tour by Langford, numerous newspaper articles, and a story in the popular *Scribner's Monthly* contributed to the limited, but increasing, body of knowledge (and folklore) about this western "wonderland." Lieutenant Doane's official report was accepted and published by Congress.

The growing publicity finally resulted in the United States government funding and supporting an official exploration in 1871. The large expedition was led by Ferdinand V. Hayden, head of the United States Geological Survey, who had been with the unsuccessful

MUD POT, VIOLET HOT SPRINGS.

Raynolds party in 1860. Hayden's purpose was to explore the region thoroughly and scientifically, and it was complemented by a simultaneous survey by the United States Army Corps of Engineers. A stunning and convincing visual record was created by noted photographer William Henry Jackson and by artists Henry W. Elliott and Thomas Moran.

BIRTH OF AN IDEA

Members of these expeditions were so impressed with the spectacle of the place that they were convinced that it should somehow be reserved for others to see and enjoy. In 1871 and early 1872, Hayden, members of the Washburn party, and others lobbied tirelessly for a congressional bill to protect Yellowstone for the benefit of everyone. Supported by the impressive imagery of Jackson, Moran, and Elliot, and following the precedent of the 1864 act that made Yosemite Valley part of the public domain, Congress enacted historic legislation. Yellowstone was officially born as the world's first national park when President Ulysses S. Grant signed the bill on March 1, 1872.

In 1886, following years of underfunded, disorganized, ineffective management, the park was officially entrusted to the care of the United States Army. During the ensuing 30 years, the army custodians accomplished much. They improved access to the park, constructed facilities (some of which are still in use), protected its features, and made early visitors more secure.

Toward the end of the first decade of the 20th Century the embryonic National Park System had grown to include 14 parks. At the urging of Secretary of the Interior Franklin K. Lane, Congress recognized the need for an agency dedicated to the administration of the parks. The National Park Service was created on August 25, 1916, and Stephen T. Mather was appointed its first director. In 1918, the fledgling agency assumed responsibilities in Yellowstone. In 1919, the first of a long series of trained, dedicated, and influential park professionals became superintendent of Yellowstone. He brought vitality, vision, and an enduring sense of direction to the park. His name was Horace Albright, and he would later succeed Mather as director of the National Park Service.

The seasons change; bison and elk and grizzlies roam the land unfettered; rainbow trout labor upstream to spawn a new generation and die; bald eagles and great gray owls swoop down on their prey; green, gray, and reddish-brown lichens cling tenaciously to rocks like reefs in Lilliput; geysers erupt in columns of iridescent steam (some more faithful than others); people come and people go; still the long march of geologic time, natural process, and human history is unfinished. The future, as always, is uncertain. But, at least for our moment in geologic time, we can be happy in the knowledge that this kingdom we treasure, and all that it is and means to each of us, is still here. We can hope that the wisdom of its wildness will endure, and we can be proud that it has been the model for similar places in more than 130 countries around the world.

CYCLES

by Lynn Wilson

GRIZZLY BEARS IN MOONLIGHT.

SPRING

Spring in the land of Yellowstone,
Is giving of old to new.
Visions, past and present,
Wet of morning dew.

Algae's vibrant colors,
Fluorescing thermals deep.
Fireweed dance thru aspen,
While flowers trace the seep.

Lakes of frigid water,
Puddles intensely hot.
Contradictions of Nature,
The living and the not.

Grass sprouts in silence,
Fragrant life bursts forth,
Swooshing feathers, a chirping nest,
Geese flying north.

Songbirds preen their feathers
In a palatial trickling pool.
Baby elk splash and play,
In rivers running cool.

Smallest of the bison,
Stampede amongst the herds.
Youthful wading moose,
Chase reluctant birds.

Swans nesting stream banks,
Reflect a regal pose.
Nary a ripple water makes,
As swiftly by it goes.

Pond lilies grace still water,
Atop their leafy mast.
While glacier lilies delicate,
Are fragilities of the past.

And I, with carnal desire,
Of Earth, water, and sky.
Embrace tranquil Nature,
Gently drawing nigh.

My human ache soon absorbed,
With fragrance of the bloom,
Murmurs of birthing trees,
And grizzlies lit by moon.

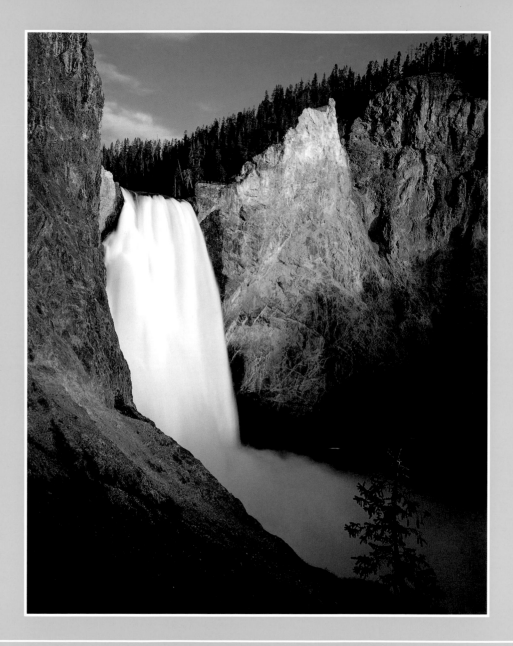

LOWER FALLS, GRAND CANYON of the YELLOWSTONE.　　　26

ASPENS & GRANITE.

CASTLE GEYSER ERUPTING.

29   LITTLE WHIRLIGIG GEYSER, NORRIS GEYSER BASIN, SUNRISE.

PINK CONE GEYSER ERUPTING.

BISON IN HAYDEN VALLEY.

RIVERSIDE GEYSER ERUPTING OVER THE FIREHOLE RIVER.

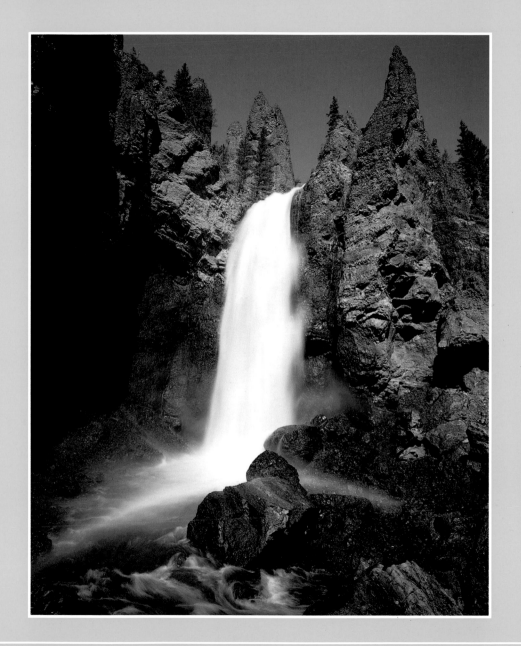

TOWER FALL & MORNING RAINBOW.

PELICAN CREEK, PELICAN VALLEY.

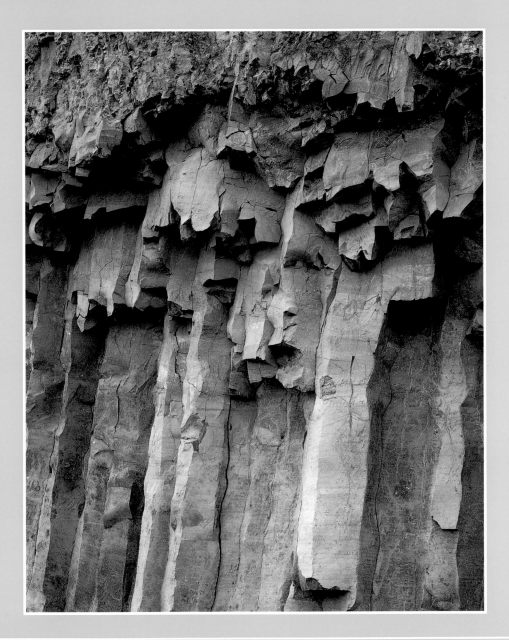

37

COLUMNAR BASALT NEAR TOWER FALL.

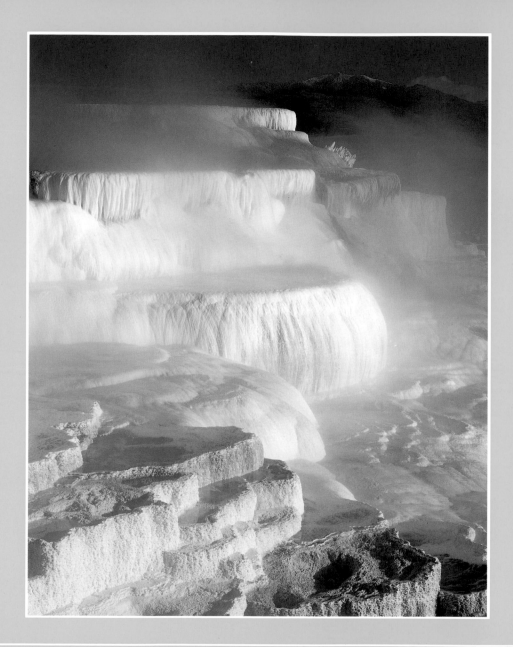

MORNING AT MINERVA TERRACE, MAMMOTH HOT SPRINGS.   38

OLD FAITHFUL, UPPER GEYSER BASIN, SPRING MORNING.

Black-tipped feathers ripple,
Glassy mid-dawn lake.
Sharp eyes seek the fish,
That pelican chicks partake.

Summer hillsides dazzle,
A tapestry of flowers.
Nature's heady umbrosia,
Feasted by me for hours.

My ears are titillated
By exploding orbs of mud,
The swoosh of spewing geysers,
Or bison chewing cud.

A hot spitter-spatter,
Like grease in a frying pan.
Erupts my quiet moment,
To pop atop the land.

Bears peek out from trees,
Pronghorns graze the green.
Bobcats print the mud,
Eyes of eagle keen.

A far flotilla of clouds,
Takes the day by storm.
Ozone mixed with sulfur,
Sprinkles Earth till morn.

Rest you Sun upon this Earth,
Thru rainbow'd fluffy clouds.
Paint pastel illuminations,
That awe quiescent crowds.

Creatures come at dusk of day,
To graze by shaded light.
Sun's asleep, moon's awake,
Chandelier'd stars of night.

GREAT FOUNTAIN GEYSER ERUPTING, MIDWAY GEYSER BASIN.

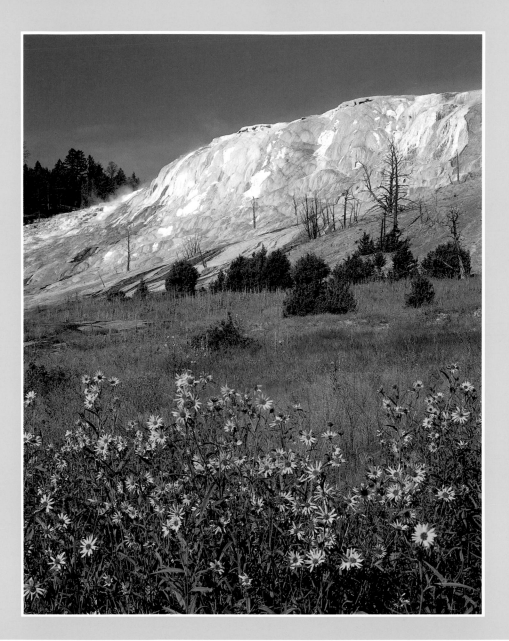

SUNFLOWERS & MARBLE TERRACE, MAMMOTH HOT SPRINGS.

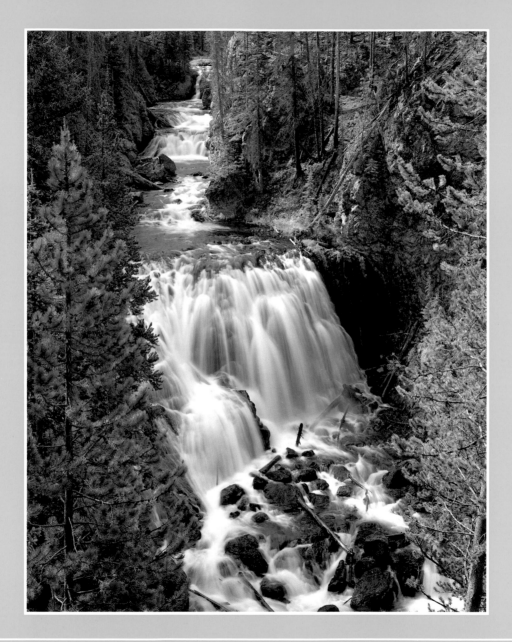

FIREHOLE RIVER AT KEPLER CASCADES.

47   GRAND CANYON of the YELLOWSTONE FROM INSPIRATION POINT.

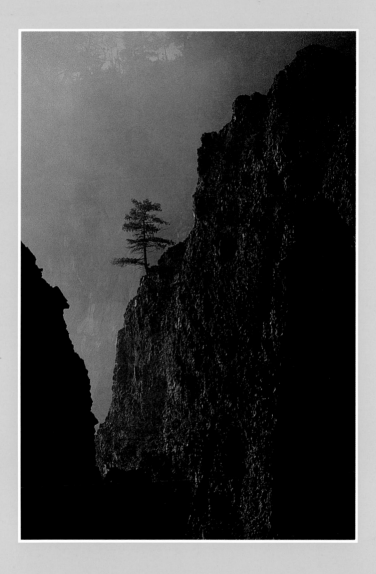

PINE & CLIFF NEAR TOWER.

LILY PADS & FLOWERS, ISA LAKE.

YELLOWSTONE LAKE, LATE-SUMMER EVENING.

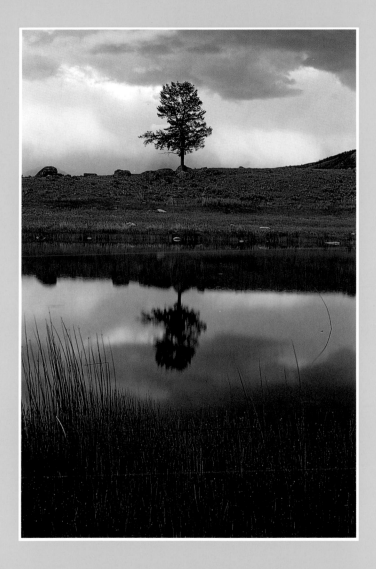

LONE TREE & GLACIAL POOL, LAMAR VALLEY, SUNSET.

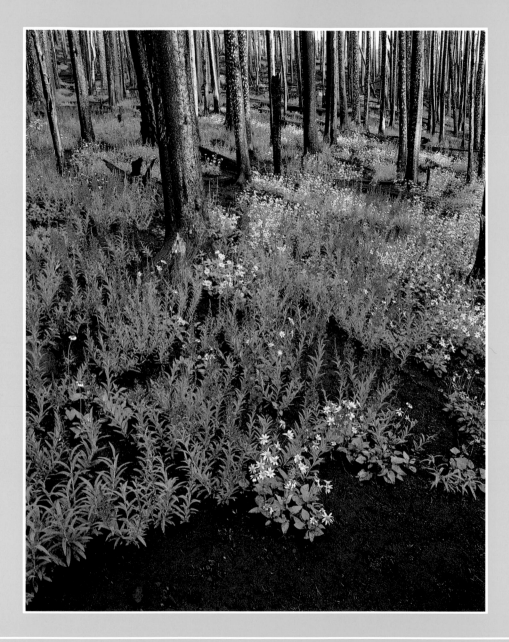

WILDFLOWERS ON FLANKS OF MOUNT WASHBURN.   54

DETAIL OF MINERVA TERRACE, MAMMOTH HOT SPRINGS.

GRAND PRISMATIC SPRING, MIDWAY GEYSER BASIN. 56

MORNING GLORY POOL, UPPER GEYSER BASIN.

AUTUMN

Riverine musky fog,
Lifts with warmth of day,
Bugling elk-filled meadows,
Beckons far away.

Massive CRACK of bighorns,
In ritualistic grace.
Vying waiting harems,
To propagate his race.

Bison gently muzzle,
To entice his current woe,
For tis rutting season,
'Til fall is mostly through.

Storms coolly quicken,
Advent of coming freeze.
Days grow short, nights are long,
Autumn-colored trees.

Rocks glow pastel,
Squirrels click the scree.
Prankster ravens glide above,
Wind-whistled trees.

Heavens fill with music,
Birds flee to be warm.
Rolls of distant thunder,
A fast approaching storm.

Lightning candles shadowed land,
White pellets begin to fall.
Visitors seeking shelter,
Watch from window'd wall.

Alone to metamorphose,
This serenely quiet place.
Snow descends abruptly,
And dons a frozen face.

YELLOWSTONE RIVER SHIMMERING IN BACK LIGHT. 60

POOL & MIST, WEST THUMB GEYSER BASIN, SUNRISE.

EVENING PRIMROSE SPRING, SYLVAN SPRINGS AREA.   62

ONE HUNDRED SPRINGS PLAIN, NORRIS GEYSER BASIN.

SUNSET LAKE, BLACK SAND BASIN, EARLY MORNING.   64

BULRUSHES AROUND THE SHORE OF SHOSHONE LAKE.

ASPENS NEAR THE LAMAR RIVER.

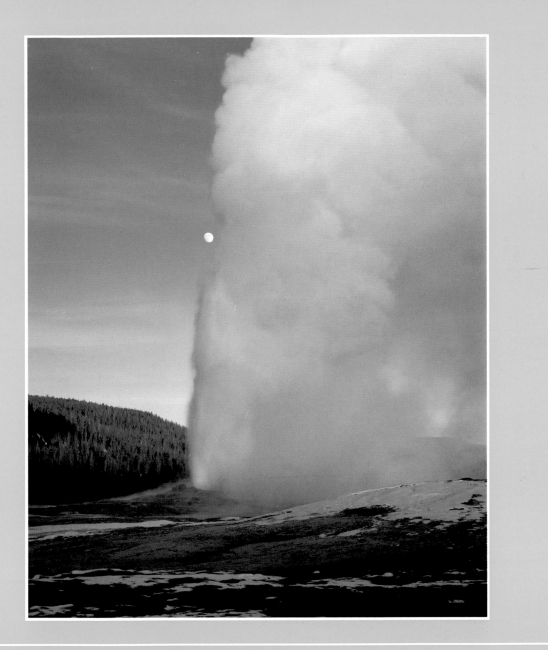

OLD FAITHFUL ERUPTING, UPPER GEYSER BASIN, MOONRISE.

YELLOWSTONE RIVER NEAR ALUM CREEK, SUNRISE.

'WICK' TREES, BLACK SAND BASIN, DAWN.

WILD GERANIUM AND STRAWBERRY LEAVES & PINE BRANCH.

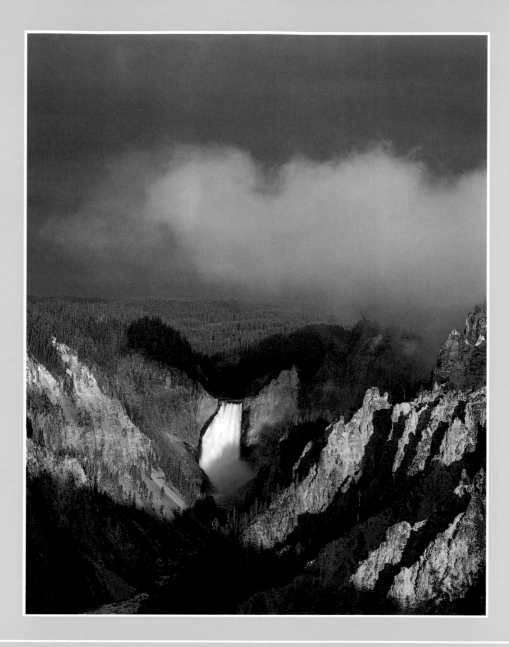

GRAND CANYON of the YELLOWSTONE, EARLY MORNING.   72

CLEPSYDRA GEYSER ERUPTING, LOWER GEYSER BASIN, SUNSET.

Waterfalls freeze mid-cascade,
Sculptured ice is born.
Frosty footprints left in white,
Azured winter morn.

Snow pack now deep,
Frozen roads are made.
Opened gates for winter,
Ski tracks soon are laid.

Cerulean sky of Solstice,
Heat of frozen air.
Joy of snow-caught aspens,
Shadowed trunks so bare.

Bursts of boiling water,
Frozen before its fall.
Blown from venting geysers,
Caught in blizzard's wall.

Captured falling crystals,
Flock a nearby pine.
Encased with frozen splendor,
Of regal winter time.

Bears lay fast asleep,
While elk roam the grounds.
Bison slowly move about,
With labored grunting sounds.

Back and forth they muzzle,
To find that blade of grass.
Minding not the people,
On snowmobiles that pass.

Skies dapple darkness,
Solar bodies hang in place.
Moonbeams sift thru snowflake's,
Prismatic lunar lace.

OLD FAITHFUL ERUPTING, WINTER DAY.

SWAN LAKE & THE GALLATIN RANGE, LATE WINTER.

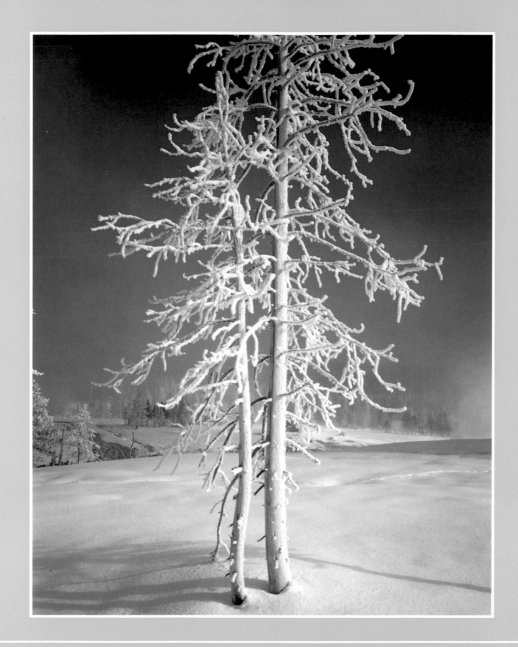

RIME ICE ON LODGEPOLE PINE, UPPER GEYSER BASIN.

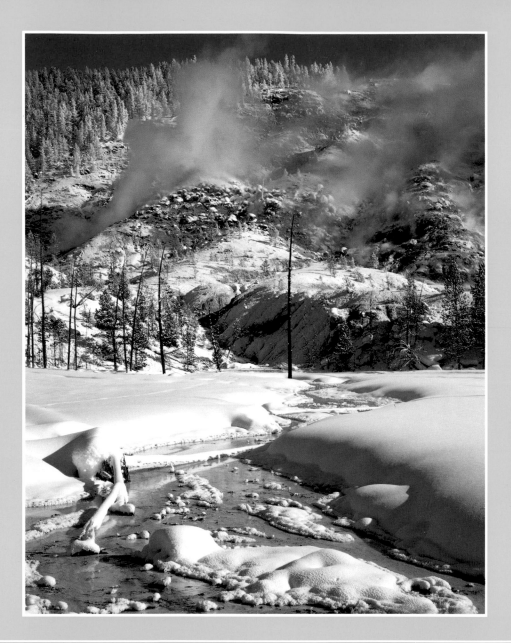

STEAM VENTS ON ROARING MOUNTAIN.

HOT SPRING, NORRIS GEYSER BASIN.

GIBBON FALLS, EARLY WINTER.

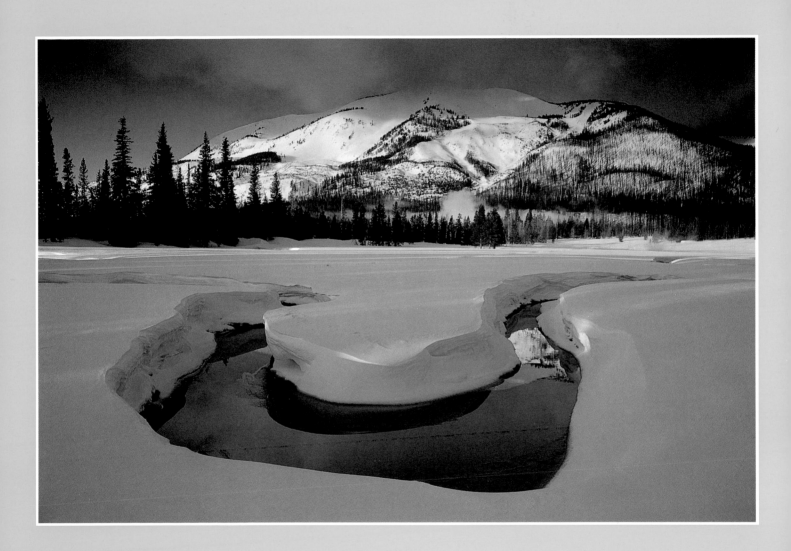

WITCH CREEK & MOUNT SHERIDAN.

CANARY SPRING, MAMMOTH HOT SPRINGS, WINTER MORNING.   84

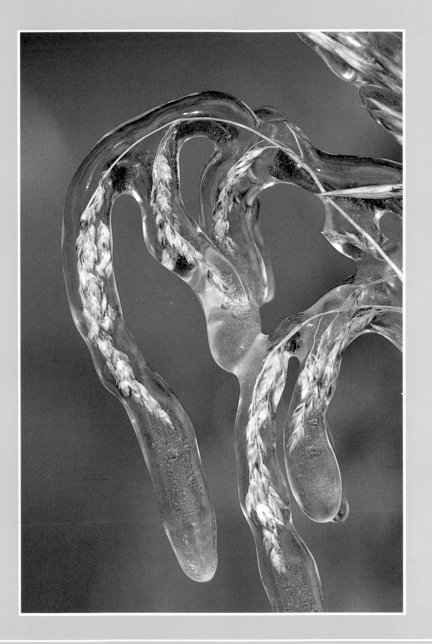

ICE COATED SEEDHEADS OF GRASS.

LAST LIGHT, MID-WINTER.

BULL ELK IN UPPER GEYSER BASIN.

FIREHOLE RIVER & UPPER GEYSER BASIN, SUNRISE.

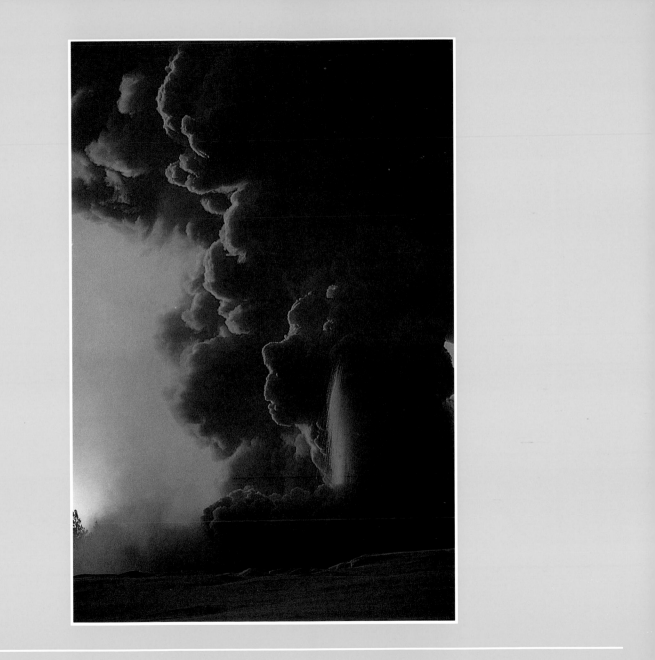

OLD FAITHFUL ERUPTING AT SUNRISE, MID-WINTER.

MOOSE CALF IN SPRING WILDFLOWERS.

Ah, 'tis spring,
With it, melt of snow.
Small streams coalesce,
As o'er the cliffs they go.

The most torrid pools,
Rich in aquamarine.
The still of yonder lake,
And edge of travertine.

Pronghorns shyly gaze,
From a lofty watching spot.
Birth of Mammoth Terraces,
From minerals in water hot.

Again spongy meadows,
Give life from latent seed.
Youngsters hungrily feeding,
On mother's milk they need.

Slowly drying soil,
Meadows richly green.
Flowers blanket hillsides,
Grizzlies rarely seen.

Eruption of Old Faithful,
Windows of our Earth.
A bird's song at daybreak,
An elk giving birth.

The innocence of babies,
Be it moose or butterfly.
Blossom painted hillsides,
Cloud puffed azure sky.

It seems to me these treasures,
Captured in my mind.
Are the touch of Nature's spirit,
To hearts of Human kind.

LOWER FALLS OF THE YELLOWSTONE RIVER. 92

BEYOND THE BOUNDARIES

by George B. Robinson

During the last decade or so our perception and understanding of Yellowstone has changed. Contrary to popular belief that it is a secure island insulated from external influence, there has been a growing awareness that the park exists in a much larger ecological context—that it is only one small part of a much larger system.

In nature, boundaries are often indistinct; they are drawn by the resources and ecological processes that link them, not by the surveyor's level and rod. Acknowledging this fundamental truth, scientists and resource managers have increasingly looked beyond the park's legal boundaries for relationships and connections. Our field of vision has been broadened to include what is called the Greater Yellowstone Ecosystem—a description that aptly conveys a sense of both the remarkable size and the outstanding significance of the area.

The wisdom of considering a Yellowstone unbound by political lines is confirmed by our knowledge that the range of the grizzly bear is nearly twice the size of the park; the migratory routes of elk, bison, and other ungulates carry them well beyond the park; and by the nature of wildland fires (like those of 1988) that move freely, and capriciously, across legal boundaries.

All ecosystems, from a miniature community of lichens

growing on a few square inches of rock to an area that includes entire mountain ranges, have edges. But, their edges are not straight, fixed, and angular; rather, like living organisms, they are soft, contoured, and subject to change. In the world of people, boundaries denote ownership, a concept that has no meaning in nature.

The Greater Yellowstone Ecosystem is an aggregation of countless smaller systems. Each is discrete and essentially self-sustaining, yet all are connected through the perpetual motion of ecological process. The greater ecosystem represents the whole organism, not just the heart. It is the larger context of life and environment in which each smaller system operates, and upon which they rely for their health and vitality.

Ecological systems import and export energy and materials with no regard for the conventional boundaries we draw on maps. The integrity of both the individual ecosystem and adjacent areas is dependent on those exchanges, or ecological subsidies. Within the system, connections are made on many pathways—the air and soil, wildlife ranges and migration routes, surface streams and subterranean aquifers, ridges and valleys, roads and trails.

With the concept of a greater, composite, ecosystem as a frame of reference, it is easier to understand how activities beyond the boundary of the national park can profoundly affect the resources within. For example, efforts to tap geothermal energy sources on private lands outside the park could seriously, and irreversibly, alter the precisely ordered conditions that give rise to Yellowstone's unique

BISON IN SNOW FLURRY, LATE AUTUMN.

geothermal features, because the underground watercourse is shared.

Toxic chemicals from upstream mine tailings could contaminate streams, lakes, and groundwater supplies. Riparian habitats could be dramatically altered, and one of the most significant natural trout fisheries in North America could be seriously affected.

Logging, oil, and gas exploration as well as sub-division and recreational development, could further fragment grizzly bear and wild ungulate habitat.

It has been suggested that as formerly continuous natural habitats (ecosystems) are increasingly fragmented by the encroachment of civilization, they begin to develop characteristics of remote islands and archipelagoes. Some ecologists have said that parks like Yellowstone are similar to land-bridge islands because most of them are slowly becoming isolated from their surroundings by habitat disturbances beyond their boundaries and, in effect, are as ecologically isolated as true islands.

In a sense, Yellowstone, and places like it, are analogs to the "commons" of 19th-century England. The concept of the commons recognized that there are some pieces of land or elements of the environment that never have been, and should never be, held in private ownership. Unfortunately, such publicly owned places often suffer what has been called the "tragedy of the commons." Each year they are shared, used, and sometimes abused by increasing numbers of common "owners." Often there is little sense of common cause for the common property. All too often lines on a map delineate adjacent areas in which inappropriate uses, or differing management

philosophies, prevail. Large ecosystems can become disarticulated because common management is not always a companion of common use.

At 2.2 million acres, Yellowstone National Park is just the core of a larger system that covers about 28,000 square miles. The challenge of establishing common management goals for this area is more clearly understood when one considers that the Greater Yellowstone Ecosystem includes two national parks, seven national forests, and three national wildlife refuges, as well as public lands managed by the Bureau of Land Management. Altogether, these federal lands total 13.9 million acres. In addition, there are 500,000 acres of state land in Wyoming, Montana, and Idaho (including land on three Indian reservations), and about 3.3 million acres of private land within the ecosystem.

For more information about the Greater Yellowstone Ecosystem, threats to its integrity, and how you can join in efforts to insure its well-being, write to:

The Greater Yellowstone Coalition
P.O. Box 1874
Bozeman, MT 59771

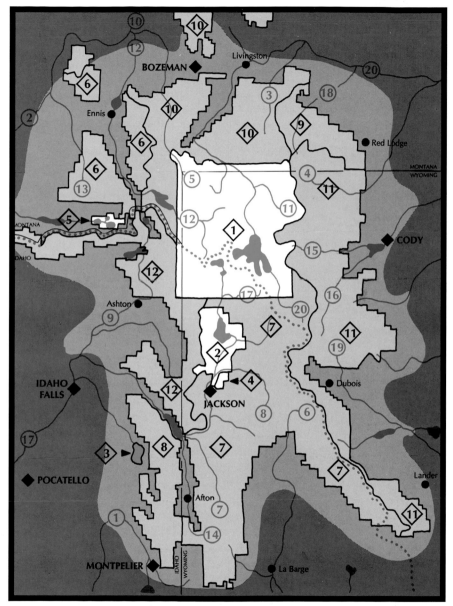

◆ FEDERAL LANDS ◆
1 -Yellowstone National Park
2 -Grand Teton National Park
3 -Grays Lake National Wildlife Refuge
4 -National Elk Refuge
5 -Red Rock Lakes National Wildlife Refuge
6 -Beaverhead National Forest
7 -Bridger-Teton National Forest
8 -Caribou National Forest
9 -Custer National Forest
10 -Gallatin National Forest
11 -Shoshone National Forest
12 -Targhee National Forest

● MAJOR RIVERS ●
1 -Bear River
2 -Beaverhead River
3 -Boulder River
4 -Clarks Fork of the Yellowstone River
5 -Gallatin River
6 -Green River
7 -Greys River
8 -Gros Ventre River
9 -Henrys Fork of the Snake River
10 -Jefferson River
11 -Lamar River
12 -Madison River
13 -Ruby River
14 -Salt River
15 -Shoshone River (North Fork)
16 -Shoshone River (South Fork)
17 -Snake River
18 -Stillwater River
19 -Wind River
20 -Yellowstone River

NORTH

GREATER YELLOWSTONE ECOSYSTEM

SUGGESTED READING

Bryan, T. Scott. *Geysers: What They Are and How They Work*. Niwot, CO: Roberts Rinehart, Inc. Publishers. 1990.

Carr, Mary and Sharon Eversman. *Roadside Ecology of Greater Yellowstone*. Missoula, MT: Mountain Press Publishing Co. 1991.

Fritz, William J. *Roadside Geology of the Yellowstone Country*. (1985). Missoula, MT: Mountain Press Publishing Co. 1991.

Glick, Dennis, Mary Carr, and Robert Ekey, eds. *An Environmental Profile of the Greater Yellowstone Ecosystem*. Bozeman, MT: Greater Yellowstone Coalition. 1991.

Haines, Aubrey L., ed. Osborne Russell's *Journal of a Trapper*. Lincoln, NE: University of Nebraska Press. 1965.

Hirschmann, Fred. *Yellowstone*. (1982). Reprint. Portland, OR: Graphic Arts Center Publishing. 1990.

Reese, Rick. *Greater Yellowstone: The National Park and Adjacent Wildlands*. Helena, MT; Montana Magazine. 1984.

Robinson, Sandra C. and George B. *In Pictures, Yellowstone: The Continuing Story*. Las Vegas, NV: KC Publications, Inc. 1990.

Wilkinson, Todd. *Yellowstone Wildlife: A Watchers Guide*. Minocqua, WI: NorthWord Press, Inc. 1992.

Wuerthner, George. *Yellowstone: A Visitors Companion*. Harrisburg, PA: Stackpole Books. 1992.

The Yellowstone Association, one of many non-profit organizations chartered by Congress to aid the National Parks, is an excellent source of affordably priced guides, pamphlets, and books. Their publications may be found in the sales areas of the Visitor Centers or by contacting them directly:

The Yellowstone Association
P.O. Box 117
Yellowstone National Park, WY 82190

PHOTOGRAPHIC CREDITS

Frank Balthis: 28,30,62. **David Blankenship:** 89. **Elizabeth M. Boehm:** 36,53. **Barbara A. Brundege:** 71,93. **Carr Clifton:** 27,35,46,79. **Ed Cooper:** 43,48. **Dick Dietrich:** 40. **Michael Francis:** 9. **Steven Fuller:** 19,78. **Jeff Gnass:** 33,39. **Jon Gnass:** 1. **Jeff Henry:** 52. **Fred Hirschmann:** 21,63,76,81,83,92. **Henry Holdsworth:** 15,23. **Lewis Kemper:** 80. **Tom Mangelsen:** 5,6,14,18,24,74. **Charles Mauzy:** 86,87,88. **Ross McCracken:** 7. **Scott McKinley:** 11,49. **Mark & Jennifer Miller:** 12. **Jeff Nicholas:** 42,57,61,64,68,70,94. **Sandra Nykerk:** 56. **Pat O'Hara:** 31,38,65. **Stan Osolinski:** 60,66,77,85. **Neil C. Ramhorst:** 58. **Diana Stratton:** 10,16,17,20,22,29,54,72,90. **John Telford:** 13,37,69. **Tom Till:** 67. **Larry Ulrich:** 26,34,44,50,73. **Jim Wilson:** Front Cover,32,47,51,55,84. **George Wuerthner:** 45,82.

CREDITS

Yellowstone National Park Map by Jeff Nicholas.
"A Place of Many Splendors" by George B. Robinson.
Geologic Time Table by Jeff Nicholas.
"Cycles" by Lynn Wilson.
"Beyond the Boundaries" by George B. Robinson.
Greater Yellowstone Ecosystem Map by Jeff Nicholas.
Hydrothermal Cross Section by Jeff Nicholas.
Edited by Nicky Leach.
Book Design by Jeff Nicholas.
Photo Editor: Jeff Nicholas.
Printing coordinated by TWP, Ltd., Berkeley, Ca.
Printed in Singapore, 1994.